Black Blossoms

Black Blossoms

Rigoberto González

Four Way Books
Tribeca

Please direct all inquiries to:
Editorial Office
Four Way Books
POB 535, Village Station
New York, NY 10014
www.fourwaybooks.com

Library of Congress Cataloging-in-Publication Data

González, Rigoberto.
Black blossoms / Rigoberto González.
    p. cm.
Poems.
ISBN 978-1-935536-15-4 (pbk. : alk. paper)
I. Title.
PS3557.O4695B63 2011
811'.54--dc22

                    2011004083

This book is manufactured in the United States of America
and printed on acid-free paper.

Four Way Books is a not-for-profit literary press. We are grateful for the assistance
we receive from individual donors, public arts agencies, and private foundations.

This publication is made possible with public funds
from the National Endowment for the Arts

and from the New York State Council on the Arts, a state agency.

Distributed by University Press of New England
One Court Street, Lebanon, NH 03766

[clmp]   We are a proud member of the Council of Literary Magazines and Presses.

in loving memory of my mother

Avelina Alcalá

(1951-1982)

in loving memory of my poet-girl

Roxana Rivera

(1977-2003)

in loving memory of the poet

Ai

(1947-2010)

CONTENTS

Part Three: Floridiez

Part Four: The Mortician Poems

PART ONE: MUNDO DE MUJERES

"how I cut through life like a diamond
in a sack of glass, with no regrets"

—Ai

WEIMAR

(after the painting by Otto Dix, *The Dancer Anita Berber*, 1925)

Strawberries are just as shameless,
    flaunting their freckles in daylight,
        making believe they entice us because
they're strawberries and not because they look like nipples.

    *

They say she knew the cut in her toe
    would start to bleed when she pressed her foot to the stage,
        her ex-lover in the front row,
seeking evidence that she still loved him.

    *

The autobiography of red begs a coda
    when the hand twitches the moment the paint
        runs out and the second hand,
the one holding the brush, provokes a stigmata.

    *

She likes her women to flush in the usual places,
    yes—the cheeks, the chest, the valley of the mound—
        but nothing tickles her more than
their palms growing warm on her back.

    *

They say she could detect a woman who had just
     miscarried by the smell of dry fruit
          escaping in the woman's breath, by the silence
in her step—a crib coming to a stop.

*

On the streets of Berlin the walls shrink back
     like stomachs kicked in and people toss
          in their sleep like forks in the sink—
all night the clanging sweats on the canvas.

*

A bath after midnight cools the burning in her calves,
     but she soaks inside another dilemma:
          will she set her throat on fire with whiskey
or with the dark-eyed neighbor?

*

The secret to the perfect angle is to use blades
     instead of bristles, is to carve a jaw
          the way one would cut into a birthday cake—
with knowledge of one's mortality.

*

They say she could bend down and suck up
      the diamond in her navel to her nostril,
            not because she was flexible, but because
she had the pull of a tornado in her nose.

*

Red, he said, because there was no other way
      to keep her still, this devil that slipped
            out of every dress except for the one
that coated her skin after her body sliced open.

*

War as Woman is what it should be called,
      this dress stretched open like a battlefield,
            this arsenal of fingertips and bullet kiss,
this bloody bed with a skull rising through it.

*

My name is Anita Berber
      and I no longer dance for anyone,
            but I'll keep my eye on you, you
who'll pirouette like smoke through the crack of the world.

for Marion Ettlinger

Black Blossoms

after Goya, Madrid

Sisters, with your grinning skulls hovering
        above the gutted stomachs of your bowls,
your teeth look so pretty when you pray.
        Say the word *broth*, say the word *mutton*

and the kitchen mocks you with dust.
        Even the cupboards have picked the teacups
clean. Say *famine* and the black magic
        of the word rewards you with resolved

conflict: dead now the old debate over poultry
        or fish—the chicken coop wireless,
the lake a sand trap that swallowed the dog.
        When the dog refused to yap at its dark

luck you tittered at its only act of bravery:
        the deliberate leap into the mud.
Poor desperate bitch, teats like beads of hardened
        wax, the dandelion of its head

jutting out in spite of its wish to forget the pity
        of you mummified mistresses,
the wooden spoons in your hands the reachable
        crucifix you split between you.

You might have eaten the dog, but it had
        three legs and you none, your femurs
long-since tapered to the floor. You stare each other
        down and laugh, consuming

the only edible resignation: humor. What is
    misery now that the last spring
you will ever know has already been forgotten?
    What is pain when the final blister

has been bitten off and broken down?
    Old widows, with your backs to the windows
you won't need light outside of your widow gowns.
    When the sun sets next it will

blossom with the blackest mushrooms and the moths
    will lay their eggs on your leathery
smiles—oh wicked wicked larvae bubbling in protein
    much too late. Isn't it funny how

whatever moves from this minute forward sets
    itself into motion without muscle?
Your hollow throats chuckle as your dimples
    digest their cheeks, as your tongues

deflate with your thighs and breasts, and as your
    bodies spasm at the last chance
for sensation: the pucker and stretch in the sutured
    centers of your gray vaginas.

MISE-EN-SCÈNE

after Lizzie Borden

You are not a woman,
    you are not a ghost,
or the shrill that makes the neighbor's hounds abort.

You are not a space between buildings,
    not wind tunnel or porthole
through which the indigent cat slips in and out of its coma.

You aren't the hermetic door with its back to the street,
    you are not the echo of the cracking wood,
or the footfalls mimicking distance

as they spiral down to the dark hole of a center.
    You are not the center.
You are not the interruption of the window

surprising the postman as he skips the tin mailbox once more.
    Every person in this house has died.
You buried your mother with a plum pit in her throat,

you buried your father without his hair or his shoes,
    you buried the hair inside the shoes.
The shoes behave like flowerpots and wait for the moss to grow.

What does a creature do
    in the tar pits of its own extinction
but lift its tusks to the heavens to pierce its own wail?

You are no less dead than the parakeet
        that gnaws at the chips of paint.
Father said to keep it in its cage

but you want something else to die before you
        hand over the room to your corpse
and disintegrate like the stack

of father's pornographic magazines in the fireplace.
        You are not the immolation,
you are not the woman pressing her shriek to the page.

But you know about turning black, limb by limb.
        You know about finding a smile
on the mantle and detached from its skull.

You buried your father without his teeth.
        You buried your father the night
he wanted to step inside you the way he enters the house.

You are not the dress
        that opens from the outside like an iron gate,
you're not the stupid woman

with her finger shoved inside her mouth.
        When she goes up in flames
she will melt into the fruit bowl.

You are not the fire, you are not the bowl.
        You are not the reason the parakeet
sputters down to the floor in a trail of smoke.

This is not your bird and this is not your house.
          You are not the screeching sirens.
No, you are not the owner—

he disappeared into the mattress and left his bones.
          You're not the daughter,
you're not the spouse.

She's in the kitchen.
          She can't get out.
You're not the poison in the soup,

you're not the knife or gun or noose.
          You're not at home.
This is not your burning house.

THE UNSUNG STORY OF THE INVISIBLE WOMAN

Phoenix, Arizona

You're the unremarkable girl who grew into the unremarkable
woman whose face eats up an inch of glass at the gas station

window, your black yawn the stillborn kiss that ushers
the five a.m. client away. If he were to turn back now

he still won't remember you since there's nothing remarkable
about your red shirt. The woman who'll replace you next week

will have been hired to wear one like it, though she will not,
like you, die inside of it. This is her story: the five a.m. client

will return in a month, she'll smile, he'll peel off her shirt
with one hand and she'll seek the scent of him haunting the walls

of her empty house, he on the road another ten nights. Pregnant
a second time, she won't forgive him his cross-country drives

and he'll watch his daughters grow like ink blots inside
the annual snapshots taken in bad light. He'll resurrect the memory

of you circa 2051 when on his deathbed he recalls
how his future wife was new there in that truck stop,

how she laughed behind the register, how she matched the ringing
of change with a bangle of religious charms. *Why so much Jesus, girl?*

he asked, and she replied: *The gal before me died last month. I think
she got shot or somethin'. Who knows what her story is? But what's yours?*

Weeping Icons

New York City

I push open the window. Pigeons blend into the stone
ledge as their small ruby hearts fade to charcoal.

Delicate as ash, they erode with the wind
and leave the white daisies of their droppings. Stranger

birds clutter the city sidewalks, their gray wings
crushed into exotic fabrics too thin for winter.

My socks are yellow cotton, the bedroom carpet
deep. I step out of my footprints easily.

From the mantel my mother weeps for me
on the day of my birth. In every other photograph

she mourns me. Her eyes melt like snow
on the street, always darkening. The Labrador

I bathed twenty years ago
snuck into my parents' room and splashed

the television screen. The pope arrived
on the Mexican peninsula to a parade

of teary-eyed saints. My mother had been
fucking a stranger beneath the sheets.

I remember that morning above any other
because that's when both my mother

and my faith began to fade. All things holy
came in chalk or plastic after that

and, too, the small god the priest placed
in my mouth finally dissolved

the night my mother greeted her final star.
When she cried out I confused the sound

with that groan of ecstasy the time I
found her with her lover. What burden to carry

her loneliness until my own demise. Motherless,
I have lived detached from the world

long enough. Should I decide to take
flight, I will die by day, divide the sky

into what will fall, what will rise. One stunned
passerby will drop a bottle of cranberry juice

on the pavement. The others will blink, surprised it
doesn't shatter, holding in the red lake in its lung.

Blizzard

Gallup, New Mexico

The heavy snow disrobes the landscape of its mountains.
I stretch a hand out the window to capture its pleasure
but it eludes my grasp because it wasn't meant for me.
Nobody knows I exist in the white month of February

and in the hungriest of hours—so ravenous they eat sound.
If there was a road it has coiled like a sleeping snake
beneath the shrinking metal of the car. I'm just as numb
in the back seat, no longer a driver. I recall that stranded

couple who survived one week on saltine crackers and body
heat. Mine is a tube of toothpaste in my bag and a man
in town who thanks me for opening my left nipple like a rose
at the prompting of his lips. When he turns his back to me

in bed his skin shades to gray and I know about the dead
who roll their eyes up to memorize the texture of their graves.
If I should freeze to death the muted explosion of my heart
will not betray me. The science of the weather will have

its own sad story to tell when I am found, ten-fingered
fetus with a full set of teeth locked to the knucklebone.
The trapped air will surrender when the door splits open
and a woman in a passing truck will romanticize my end.

Did I escape or was I abandoned? Either way I take no
possessions with me, unless I open my mouth and name
my tongue a possession. A slippery wedge of a muscle, it
shifts like solid stone in the arctic of my jaw. The word

that swam to my throat, that word, *love*, grows thick
with ice like everything that keeps me company tonight:
my lung at sub-zero, my empty heart—those pieces of the body
that cannot thaw but shatter at the touch of heat.

DEAD WOMAN'S JEWELRY AT AN ESTATE SALE

Cuernavaca/New York City

Mrs. Drummond summons up a cemetery
for the woman who owns the earrings she's about to buy.
She's an old woman too and she knows about

the clutter of hooks, wires, beads. Stones
like these don't even fool themselves and wear
the adhesive off in public parks, where the scavenger birds

pick at their senseless vanity. The dead lady
left behind so much jewelry yet Mrs. Drummond
suspects she was buried with modest studs because

here she stands before a mirror, modeling the gaudier
legacy of her collection. A woman like this,
whose closet cascades belts with lackluster buckles,

no longer reigns supreme over a kingdom of sequins
and glitter. The retired army of her mules and flats
rejects the discipline of symmetrical formation.

Mrs. Drummond might have seen her on the street
some months ago, before her death, a pale lady spending
her strength to hold up a white wig, and Mrs. Drummond

might have smirked, knowing she would outlive her,
a small accomplishment no doubt but one of the few she has
left—that and picking out a matching pair in silver

to compliment that white blouse she brought back
from Cuernavaca, a place with a *camposanto*, where
white people were buried as long as sixty years ago,

their names—Moreland, Lacey, Hart—no longer foreign,
but right at home among the mauve and peach mausoleums,
cherubs with clipped wings, a tile so blue it invites

the beetles to dip their suckers for a drink. She strolled
along the faith of tombs, peeked through the windows
of wreaths, traced the odd writing on stone. Even the spear-

headed gladiolus looked baroque in its sparse flowering;
she might have seen similar sadness on a Tarot card.
And yet there was festivity in every upright monument

as if nobody took death lying down. There is where
a collector of bright things belongs, sunning her entire
grave above ground. After all this rummage Mrs. Drummond

decides on a pair shaped like seashells. She feels a draft
and amuses herself: has she fooled the dead woman's husband's
ghost, enough to make him whisper in her ear because

she brought back from the dead an owner for these earrings
for another month or two, perhaps a year? As she buys
her basketful of trinkets, Mrs. Drummond takes comfort

in knowing that death appreciates the flashy cloth
and ornate metals down in México. When her skull bleeds
through her scalp, south is where she too will want to go.

for Mahsa Hojjati

THE BALLAD OF LUCILA LA LUCIÉRNAGA

Tijuana-Mexicali, Baja California

Mine is a familiar tale: I ran away with the circus.
When the trapeze artist swung from platform to platform,
a hole in the tent his elusive halo, I knew the devil's

mischief was at work and I had no choice
but to leave my bed-ridden father without filling
his water pitcher or emptying the bedpan or singing his lullaby

the way I always said I would should the prince
in his storybook tights leap out of the pages and into
the humid afternoons of a border town so dark with people one

more moribund shadow makes no news. Headlines come
from this: a circus caravan plunging into the gulf of la Rumorosa—
canyon steep as the depths of the imaginations

that immortalized the ghosts there. Vehicles collect
at the pit like the discarded shells of uncooked shrimp.
When the gray elephant trunks drop limp among the chimps

cracked opened like coconuts, the mad poet fits the oddly-
shaped cadavers into the lines of my song. Lucila la Luciérnaga,
young girls will weep at my tragedy and never leave

their fathers or else they risk my fate—whinnying for all
eternity's midnights like the orphaned fillies found roaming
among the rubble for phantoms. Could I defend myself

I'd say that splattering into the four directions was just
more places to go. *Only joking, girls.* My humor was
the first gift of my freedom, reclaiming laughter my father

took from me each time he beat me when he couldn't beat
his wife. When my mother died, I knew my day would
come to seek a life, and found it with circus folk who understand

the romance of stallion courtship, the elegance of lions licking
at their furry knuckles after mating. To make love among
the beasts is to lie across the dreamscape of animal passion,

where every whimper, every grunt finds a body and creates
motion. My lover called me *firefly* by the way my buttocks
lit up at the height of excitement as he took me from behind.

I wore a skirt with lights after that, guiding the horses
with a wand around the ring. Lucila la Luciérnaga, the audience
called me, and my lover winked from the highwire.

As the circus wagons rolled down the canyon, no different
from cages suddenly, my lover placed his hand on my ass,
a complicit touch that said this was the fall without a net,

exactly as he dreamed it nights before when he awoke
to the groan of the bear giving birth. He reached over to insert
his fingers in me as he said: *Lucila, baby, please turn off the light.*

The Girl with No Hands

after the Brothers Grimm

Your father asked for more than a polka-dot tie,
    a self-portrait in Crayola
or cinnamon snickerdoodles flat as candle stubs

on the baking sheet. He grabbed you
    by the wrists and severed your hands
to wear on his key chain like a pair

of lucky rabbit's feet. What's so
    fortunate about a rabbit hopping
about the prairie with a missing limb?

What if all four of its legs had been clipped?
    It eats only as far as it can stretch
its neck, and then rolls itself on its back

to perforate its starved belly with the blades
    of its ribs. When the hunter returns,
the rabbit will have its revenge, looking like

the amputated foot of his diabetic mother
    wearing that familiar bunny slipper.
Your father seized your hands, not out

of malice, but greed—his wish to match
    Midas and pocket the small golds of his
kingdom—Rolex, wedding bands, crucifix,

and the precious treasures of your rings, which,
        little princess, will never leave
your fingers because Papi breaks no promises.

He never abandoned you either,
        always there when you see the hairbrush,
perched on the bristles like a nesting pecker.

Resolute, you age with ingenuity, learning to eat
        right off the branch, nibbling apple, apricot
and pear without separating fruit

from stem. This is how you heard about
        the clever rabbit, from the hunter's son
who made love to you pressing his fists

to the small of his back. He locked you
        against the tree trunk and your shoulders
splintered the bark. What a miracle

of an instrument, the piano that's played
        with elbows and knees and four clumsy
heels that for all their random reaching make

the sweetest rhythms. Your bodies
        danced each afternoon in the grove
while your mother sewed the mysterious

tears in your dresses. You forgave your mother's
        inactivity that night when Papi struck
down your wrists with a cleaver, the mirror

of the metal like a window to a furnace,
        the shadow puppet butterfly emancipated
finally. Who knew chopped bone could sing?

Maybe chicken doesn't utter a note at its
        beheading because its mother
hen isn't near to cluck a frenzied requiem.

Your mother squealed as fiercely as a
        sow and your stumps looked like the bloodied
snouts of swine. But all that rage escapes

you now as you unleash the power of the hand
        your father left intact, and with it grip
your lover tighter into you. So this

is delectable defiance, Miss Rabbit—
        it must have been a female to claim
the last word. You, girl with no hands,

can produce another pair and more:
        legs, torso, head, and a bear trap of a jaw
to bite the hands that feed her.

THE BEAUTY OF GUANAJUATO

A woman knows her husband's secret pleasures. My father's
were slips. When I saw him through the keyhole, swinging

his hips like a hula girl I couldn't wait to tell my mother.
And then I saw her foot tapping out a rhythm from the bed.

I wondered how they had reached that moment, he
confessing his passion for silk stretched across his bare crotch,

she indulging him since his penis had fattened like the clock's
weight when he hiked up the skirt just before sex. That night

flickers like a reel of film especially now in my own
bedroom, with my own husband neglecting to touch me again.

How to coax him into speaking his desire? Like this: lifting
his lip as he sleeps, I uncover the need that presses his tongue

against his teeth. Oh stealthy detective, I know that scent
of rigid earth that flies out when he whistles. So I shadow him

to the underground museum, the mummies posing like
department store mannequins. He stands for hours like the dead

reflection of the dead woman in a velvet dress. She, a true
Catrina with her gums receding to affect a smile. Her fingertips

soiled as if she had dug herself out of the ground. What amuses him?
The hands that he can snap in half like crackers, the leathery flesh

that he can peel back as easily as a tangerine's, or the sunken
eye pits staring out like assholes? I must admit she's quite a beauty,

this dead thing that poses like a lady, her spine braced with pride.
The left toe pokes out like the nose of a mouse and I feel the urge

to kiss it. My husband must be wishing the same since once
he craved the accidental gift of my wrist exposed between

coat sleeve and glove. This dame is full of secret blessings:
a missing button at the top of her blouse reveals the unbridled

ends of thread; the opened collar provides a glimpse of the valley
of the delicate neck; and in the neck itself grows the root-like

architecture of wrinkles and bone. I step into the light,
approach my husband from behind and join him on the glass,

three cadavers stacked in a communal grave, encased in an orgy
of stopped breath. I place my hand on his shoulder. He splits

my fingers with his thumb. The dumb corpse grins with complicity
as if she knows, oh yes, she knows, that she has joined these

two other people in bed. Husband runs his knee to lift her dress.
Wife invites the bristly skin to rub and rub against her skin.

Thinking Stones

She said stones are capable of thought. They had to be:
any object with sound could think. Something about

the waves trapped inside of rock, memory of time.
Something about rock's metallic viscera. The Japanese

had it right, cultivating a contemplation garden on a bed
of sand fluid as blood, each rock electric as a brain, she said.

Dementia brought out the poet in your mother.
I sit at her side writing down what intrigues her: horses,

because they wear a fifth hoof over the mouth; flashlights,
because they can't keep secrets; and stones.

Lately, even the gravel has been buzzing with collective
thought: death, the last mystery of what has crushed

all else beneath its weight. My mother pities that,
and comforts a stone in one hand. I remember

my own soft fist inside her fingers years ago, when
my mother could roller skate and guide me

through the shaky sidewalk. When she laughed, I imagined
doves in flight, seed puffs escaping through the fence,

and everything else that ascends toward light. My mother
doesn't keep her days of wonder, nights of anguish anymore.

I think fossil, I think watermark, about the stubborn
barnacle that makes a tomb of its home. The woman

next to me is the place of my birth and she will free me
to wander the shifting plates of the planet on my own.

She can leave without me, deaf to my cries, my pleas,
my fear of getting locked out of her house. I must stand

before the apathetic windows. No use knocking on the door.
I think sleeping oyster, think coma, think stone.

FLOR DE MUERTO, FLOR DE FUEGO

Los Angeles

Cempoalxóchitl. Marigold. Flower,
the scent of cold knuckles delights you, as does

the answer to death's riddles:
What's the girth of the hermit tongue once it retreats

into the throat and settles like a teabag?
What complaints do feet make when they tire of pointing

up and fold flat like a fan of poker cards?
Where do the dead hide the humor of the ass crack

when the buttocks unstring their fat?
When you sprung into the earth, all other colors coughed

and gave you the gift of sick-bed
sullenness and the contagious texture of tragedy:

Once there was a widow who exchanged
her heart for your head, but you outgrew her body,

protruding from her chest like an unsightly tumor.
Despite that she carried you, cradling you in her hand

during mass, a solace in the memory
of her husband's scrotum. If she heard a hymn

in your petals it was the sound
of trousers unzipping. If she could name the smell inside

the folds of your corolla,
she kept the word wet against her tongue. The widow

held you tighter then. So you stung her
palm in protest and then crumbled when she flung you

like a shooting star—
all awesome arc and damned glory of evisceration.

To pay her back you pierced the shivering
heart she left balanced on your stem. You loved her

all over again because she turned
yellow with death, because she was like you,

something dry to come undone
in pieces in the pitted ground. Flor de muerto, flor de fuego,

you humble down life
to the last ember. Even the phoenix tired of sewing

its bird bones together
and couldn't outlive you, oh mortality muse, oh end.

for Maythee Rojas

Widow

Don't you dare remove your black dress:
the sound of a garment mourning the loss

of your body's comfort will break our hearts.
Pity the closet and its communion of hurt—

anemic blouses, slacks thin with hunger,
an evening gown left to wonder

if her dinner date will ever materialize.
Mama, if you're naked there will be less

of you to love. Already you walk around
hollow as the alley now that your husband's

dead. Your eyes, like the alley's puddle,
cannot hold on to light and must settle

for the fleeting faces of strangers.
They flash in passing. None will linger.

for Amelia Lira Madrigal

Part Two: Floreo

"I would like to think that no one would die anymore
if we all believed in daisies"

—Anne Sexton

Frida's Wound

for Halima, the girl without grandmothers

Floriuno

Orquídeas

Your life began this way, with the dream of orchids, bone-white, gristle-
like, pollinated by flies. Then again, life ends this way as well: with flowers,

the smallest regrettable sacrifice. In the dream, you are not the orchid,
or the fly, you are the shadow in the flower's funnel—the line of darkness

that withdraws into itself like the crab pulling its exoskeleton back. A fly
laps at the petal with its needle-tongue. That is not death but the knowledge

of death, the prosaic detail an important one eventually. Then what is death?
The orchids themselves? The dream? Neither. The orchids are simply orchids,

the beauty and the grief of life. Every flower that blooms implodes: aromas
are the legacy of ghosts. The dream is voice finding its throat. Have you ever

seen sound? The whiteness of the orchids, the fly, the shadow draining down
to the shaft—all of this is sound. Did it not travel to your mother's bed

and into the fever of your sleep? And the dream—it means the fear of exiting
the womb and of entering mortality. Arrival means death.

Floridós

Cruz de Sal

A cross drawn with brine banishes north winds. A cross built of stone
extradites women. You've seen pictures of your grandmothers' graves

and dreamed God's colossal hand twisting the stones like wind-up keys
as your grandmothers rise into grace like ballerinas. One wears a rose

in her hair; the other what looks like a rose, except it cries a cherry tear.
A kiss your grandfather planted in her ear will change love's consistency

forever. Wednesday ash indicts you for inheriting the dark Catholic
complexions. Like the women before you, you seek redemption in the stoic

crucifix. A pious life is the long rehearsal of eternal rest: sleep, sickness
and salvation find you level to the ground. When you stretch your arms out

you are chiseled flesh, and the cross most likely to pity the women
whom prayer failed. One dropped her heart and it scattered like an unstrung

rosary, the other emptied her skull like a leaking grail. They're hinged
on transparent crosses with plumes of blood, swirl of fluids in a clear syringe.

Floritrés

Santuario

Hummingbirds have come to gossip to the blushing hibiscus: across the bay
another capsized ferry. Drifting bodies stiff as planks will repeat the same

story all week. The bereaved will wait, silhouettes of gulls along the bank,
knowing the dead seek land for their hands turned anchors. By evening,

mosquito frenzy. Your mother, stung, lies on the surf, her mind expunging
murky thoughts. Is she among the living or the dead? Is hers the mouth

housing the silver eel of a tongue? Or are hers the bored eyelids, thick
as clam shells, pushing the sun back into the sea? Her mother has just died,

she is neither, she is both. Orphans learn the comfort of a catatonic state
from suckling death out of nipples. They forgive their mothers for the mocking

skulls beneath their faces. They will wander the earth with placentas
instead of hearts. Ask your father, exile who wept for his wife when she rose

from the ocean, slick and wet as the baby she brought into the world,
both of you wailing the song that women sing when one of their own returns.

Floricuatro

Baby's Breath

Every birthday you eat a year off your mother's life—your mother plucked
in parts, petal by petal like the schizophrenic daisy, stares down as her heart

bubbles out vulnerable as yolk. The needle-thin rays of the sun
press against her every morning when she opens her mouth to yawn

and exposes the waking weevil of her tongue. What is it about mothers
that makes them so mortal? Is it that every mother bleeds? Is it that every

mother weeps into the jaundiced rags of her hands after the bodies she hums
into the world exclude her? Yes, you'll leave her, first memory of your gums.

She slumps among the furniture and marvels at the temporary power
of populating houses. Skin and wood, these are the archives of your hours.

The floor maps footsteps with cracks on the tile. Your mother records
the sounds of her sleepless nights. This is what keeps her alive

for now: the sleepwalk through the walls as she lactates through her robe,
your baby breath settling like the snowdrift in a dusty water globe.

Floricinco

Doppelgänger

There once lived a girl who sang and danced even in times of sorrow.
She didn't answer to your name, but before her death she wore your face,

mask bequeathed to her as well. Like you, she inherited her small place.
Such expediency of selection: the pasty stars collapsing to allow

the other constellations room to expire into brightness. But you needn't
share her fate. You can live an entire life without succumbing to a flood:

you can hum without gurgling beetle mud, you can sway without shivering
neck-deep in tin debris. But borrowed body, in time you must vacate,

let another take your space. Don't worry about whom or when since the girl
who comes after is already here, her breath the cold carnation of frost

on the window as you press your reflection to the glass. When you die
you'll kill the girls you used to be. As you live, you'll flaunt the genocide

like lavender, fierce blossoming of beauty and mortality. The next assassin?
She's the winter rehearsing its inhale-exhale through the invisible nose.

for Omaira Sánchez

37

Floriséis

Sleeping Murders

Illusion of sleep where the dead forget to keep still. The poppies
of their eyes take to the light and melt like crayons. Palette skulls.

You dip a finger in your grandmother's socket and paint
the scarlet back into her cheeks. Invent a name for this resurrection:

floreo. Minutes from now your awakening will murder every
flower in your head and you'll be none the wiser. Your great-

grandmother was an exquisite gardener and when she died her tulips
burst like swallows on the wire following the report of the gun. Dumb

birds, dozing with moth-cramped gullets, the down drifting off into
another dream. Bisabuela, magician before her death: give her a mirror

and she'll multiply parakeets in the cage, give her a flea-ridden dog
and she'll extract from a mutt an exotic Dalmatian. Give her a girl

who sleeps inside the coffins of her foremothers and she'll plant
perennials near the crib to teach her how to bring back the dead.

Florisiete

Fear of Shadow Puppets

Charcoal homunculus that only his five-fingered mother can tame
by closing the socket to seal his hunger's glare. Still he longs

for texture and seeks out the meat of depth, the elusive third
dimension denied him the moment he crawled into life, bastard

child of flesh and light. No wonder he's cruel, finding kinship
with the knuckle of rock, mimicking stings vulgar as black flower

wasps. But even as he triumphs on walls he will bow to his mentors—
your hands. The day you smothered the baby rabbit, its frightened face

expelled from the skull, your mother knew you had been pledged
to cold humanity. The sock-limp creature dropped to the tile and screeched.

No, that wasn't the dead rabbit that was you in your range of explosion:
shock, confusion, fear, and grief. What crude consolation: a changeling,

antennae-eared with a twitching transparent snout. Painful reality:
you won't ever sit on that couch again without a ghost on your knee.

Floriocho

Los Disfraces de Frida

Expletive, flower: spine supple as a stem, nose crushed into the white
corolla, profile flat as a postcard, cicada eye. Pubic hair, roots: lady,

you will always know how to squat. The bus revs its rattling engine
as it waits among the rows of your corneas. Perhaps forethought

is a female trait. Wear these other costumes next: gypsy, medium, witch.
Intuition. In family myths, your grandmother knew before marriage

that her husband would outlive her by twenty-four years. Vision in fever
during adolescent menstruation. Not hallucination, not dream as she

sat on a blue grave, watching her children wail. She knew they were hers
by the wilted lilies on their clothes. She knew she was dead by the smell

of trapped alcohol and salt—all corpses wiped cleaned that way. Her solace
was she'd never breast-feed any daughters. But deep inside the echoes

of the future fetus kicking, she sensed one of her sons would chromosome
a girl: oh ticking talisman, oh exalted seer of the sorrows yet to come.

Florinueve

Death by Morning Glory

Love vine. Strangleweed. Cribs hug their infants to the point
of suffocation. The startled cat springs into the sewage pipes and takes

her own life. Perhaps you shouldn't have touched her while she napped,
her tail sleep-stirring a ripple of heat in the air. Remember the bunny?

Every word in your mouth is a taste of the bittersweet lessons: glass,
bee, pepper, match—all pretty sounds ablaze. Dip your toe in the coal

and learn something more. Like your kind, you'll feel your way through
excursions and bleed to death. But that's existence: the opposite of coma.

Even the hornet aims to release its single drop of fire before getting crushed
into the window sill. Small legacy of the senses. Everything wants to leave

its mark in the world. Morning glory, tentacle, lovely lilac, how it pleases you
to be reckoned with in the garden. Girl, don't ever scar without a story

for your mother to tell as she walks into the parlor where the childless
go. Let her stand proudly when she says in old age: *I had a little girl once...*

Part Three: Floridiez

"Su corazón se iba llenando
de alas rotas y flores de trapo."

—Federico García Lorca

Vespertine

Stop-breath, stop-time, stop-world, steering wheel.
    Those who don't drive solo don't know
about the only lane a day from midnight on a road so lonely
    it considers transit company.

The zero of the hour darkens tunnel-socket
    right behind the car and always the winking
cyclical theater of the path just ahead. The bloodshot mirrors
    hypnotize and never a question

about how tree shadows operate without the puppeteer.
    Though suddenly nothing has strings
attached—not the croupy voice rattling the dashboard,
    not the pedal-pushing anvil-foot,

not the fingers tap-tapping a devil's tattoo.
    Even the watchdog moon, so bored with the old
story of a single unit forcing light to the eye-stinging minutes
    of yawn, unhinges its coat

and hops off its stool. Without the moon,
    the night has turned its black. Without the moon,
the moth flattens its crêpe against the windshield
    to rub its prayers against glass. What parade

this? A word on a young woman's tongue, a word
    at her fingertips, a word inside her ear.
But if she's alone was there ever language? Simple mercies
    love silence though the engine

has its own sordid tale, a once-upon-a-sight,
a happily-never-after, all device and no plot.
Scratch that, cancel that, backtrack—
the young woman's mind reverses the jump-start:

gas up and begin again.
Stop-breath, stop-time, stop-world, steering wheel.
Those who don't drive solo don't know
about the sensuality of midnight, coy as an evening gown,

as a plunging neckline, as gloves
that seduce the arms to the elbows. Knees apart
on the vinyl seat and a voyeuristic mirror
waiting for the naked lips to dance beneath its oils.

And suddenly everything has beauty mark
status—the windshield night-bathing its chest
of white freckles, the hood pushing forth
the trophy of its traffic scar, the smoky skirt

sprouting diaphanous blossoms in lieu of the spill
of a dirty martini. Even the bristly moon,
in dire need of a thorough exfoliation, unhooks
its bathrobe and heads for the spa. What lights

of fancy this? Cassiopeia sending her five-spoked
vanity from above? Without the moon to out-shout her,
she can call to the pretty girls below. Without the pretty girls
the country thickens like the gulfweed

over the Sargasso Sea.
        Road where the dead end snakes through the dark
with its stomach stretched, won't let the buoy
        catch in its throat. A room offstage is waiting

for direction; all of its corners costumed
        in kohl. But what if the actress never shows?
Does the production close? The cloud rafters
        unfurl into complaint and the cardinals bubble like blisters

when they hear their moan. Ladies
        and woodsmen, drop your violets, asters
and toothworts on the prairie floor. And the wolf
        will not startle and the moon will keep its O.

And the daybreak will evaporate its sorrow.
        And hunters will aim for the elk and watch
the curves of its flanks erase themselves
        from the canvas striped with autumn oak. And the breeze

will caress the meadow as if the ripple
        of sound has nowhere else to go. How fortunate
the thinking wishful that they can instruct
        a landscape of prose that rises to the roof and never tumbles—

not even when it shatters its hip.
        This is the part where the young woman enters.
This is the part where she leaves. Her life
        so quick it could have been missed had she left

no evidence for the blackbird to construct
        its nest. Collector of pity things, what synecdoche
makes your chickadees mourn to chirp?
        Tweets the beak: a fiber bending like a Mississippi estuary,

memory of a blouse a woman wore
        to dance with her beloved father . . . when sun
the warmth of pacific waters, when wind
        the chime of México. When dusk

the ghost of a thousand feathers of winter migrations now
        unborn. Exquisite exhale, spiral of snuff
that drills its point into requiem. Rosary seeds
        too trapped in pit to ever split. Sad privilege

of priestly pronouncements, pious excessive
        for boot-to-the-cobblestone girl. Gear-shifter, word-sifter,
what destination next? What razored
        poem? At journey's end when every paper

hearkens back to bark, and every word unspools
        itself unspoken, and every kiss and wound unpeels
to soon-forgotten, and every skid mark
        tapers off, here in the cage of my cold cold coffin

grief of your death is the shriek shriek shrieking
        hare in the woods, solitary pulse that inks in
the absolute darkness from my pen to my pain pain painful
        wheel steering, world stopping, time stopping, breath-stop.

for Roxana

Part Four: The Mortician Poems

"Death is a Dialogue between
The Spirit and the Dust.
'Dissolve,' says Death – The Spirit 'Sir
I have another Trust' –"

—Emily Dickinson

The Mortician's Scar

Purely comical, his mother's leaving, her buttocks balanced
on the narrow vinyl of the bicycle seat. He nearly giggled
at the memory of the pack-mule, its burden of sacks of grain,

but that is how she zoomed right out of his life, quickly
shrinking down to a stutter through the roads he was never
allowed to explore on his own. The house was a maze of rooms,

too many to count in one afternoon, so he watered the garden
until he gutted the soil of worms. The flowerpots pissed
defiantly on the wall. And he might have emptied the land

of water, made the sleeping Sierras cough with thirst,
had his father not arrived to turn the knob. He spanked him well
into the night and it was good to blame his father's hand for the pain.

If only it had bruised his mother's cheek with whiskey, tugged
at the black weed of her braid, or even wandered through
the softer-scented alleys of the street. His mother's absence

was the puzzle that his father's presence couldn't explain.
What does the moon mean without his mother? Just another
empty mouth in the world. What is *he*? Pity that dissolves

on the neighbor's tongue like salt. Where is his father?
His father turns in bed and reaches out to occupy the second pillow,
pinches his own penis until he can't forget the hard touch

of every night that came before. But he, a boy six years away
from playing man, no matter how long he fondles it's always
that same briny odor. He shoves the taste of it, the sting of it,

Mami's midnight suckler memory of it to his own hot mouth and...
faults himself for having lost what once must have been so sugar
sweet, so pleasing to his mother. But no matter where she's gone

she took what's rightly his with her—the bicycle, his getaway
gift from Papi the week after the dogs ran rabid. The bite on his calf,
the painful shots, the scar that twitches to the ghost of russet fangs

was worth a bicycle that could outrun the fastest mutt.
And Mami learned to drive it first. She spun around the block,
then two, then three, then promised that the next time she would

come for him. *So you just wait, my son, just wait for me.*
I'll be right back, my little man, my secret on two pigeon-toed
feet, my crippled warrior, victim of the brown bitch.

THE MORTICIAN'S BRIDE SAYS *I'M YOURS*

The city of tremors and toxins can't have
enough parlors waiting patiently along the street like
the bald-eyed scavengers who profit from the art of waste removal.

How fortunate I am—betrothed to the mortician's protégé.
On Thursday nights he drives up with the hearse,
and while every dog panics and every doña checks the mirrors

for the reaper's breath, I dab perfume inside that soft
warm space behind my bra. There, where the armpit meets
the breast, my lover yearns to find the scent of violets.

I'm all discoveries tonight: inside my shoe, Sor Juana's bill;
a flea bite pimpled on the knuckle of my thumb; a sickle-
shaped scratch at my ankle—the swift-broom

accident that greeted me this morning when I thought
I heard a voice behind the drapes. The voice itself
didn't frighten me as much as the fact that I replied.

Your name, the voice demanded. *Marisol,* I said,
shocked immediately at how easily I gave my name away,
my mouth the owl's niche after the tender hatchling

of my tongue plopped out. Sound is death because it's
irretrievable and every time I speak I die a little more.
As I rub my foot with oil I also mourn the pain

slowly vanishing. It's one more precious possession gone.
Oh the devastating truth of loss, oh mercy. I have been
parting with myself since birth. My baby teeth,

my baby fat, that babble and lisp, all gone.
Every third month two inches of my hair disappears,
every second week the tips of fingernails. Plucked eyebrows,

skin scabs, saliva, menstrual blood—I'm losing pieces
of my body constantly; nothing's mine exclusively.
Like my hands. They belong to the broom. My feet

to my shoes. The legs are the property of destinations.
My womb of my progeny. My face takes shape
only when the bedroom grants me permission to emerge.

Whatever parts are left I offer to my lover
on a pastry dish. How he pecks and pecks, that hungry crow,
on the morsels of my flesh. How he devours me,

and every bite and nibble leaves a little less to call
my own. *You're mine*, he says, and means it. *Go to him*,
says the bedroom. *Take his hand*, says the broom. In the end,

all of me belongs to this mortician. And he knows this,
presumptuous bastard, by how he holds his fingers out
and guides my way into the narrow cushions of his hearse.

The Mortician's Mother-in-Law Says Goodbye

At 70 you're still capable of the grief that wipes
its tears away with both fists. The sadness of little girls
never grew old in your eyes or in your throat—how it

hiccups rehearsing the same melancholy sounds.
Sorrow, you have learned, is two-fingered: V-shaped
it shuts your daughter's eyelids, adjoined it blesses

forehead, heart, shoulders, lips. Your granddaughter chased
another child around her mother's coffin and the loose
ribbon on her waist made you cry because the white bow

it once was was your creation and what a brief life it had.
The scissors, seamstress, that cut the shrouds of many,
lay cold as a pair of bovine nostrils widening against

barbed wire. You saw the cow freeze to death that winter,
and when she died she died standing, stubborn to the end
that old hide, drawn to your window by that flickering lamp—

a discard from your son-in-law's parlor.
Perhaps she had the power of the third eye, mesmerized
by the ghostly shadows of the blue hands drawn to the warmth

like moths. When the dead hold the light they
realize it is what is not them and they begin to love
the darkness that is. Old woman, you surprise yourself

tracing the last touch of your daughter's hand. It was here,
on your left breast. An awkward place, but it was not
the first time it had felt her grasp. When she suckled

55

as an infant it was there she reached for first, the warm milk
leaking from the raw button of your nipple. The ache
comes back to haunt you and you push it off discreetly

with your elbow. You wonder if this is how the body
begins to die, remembering its courtship of contact
and desire, moving memory back to the first sensation.

Then your daughter is here inside of you now, pressed
against the pink walls of your uterus. Slowly she
escapes you, unpeeling foot, skull and spinal cord—

you're feeling clawed, stomach turned, insides shredded.
And just as you're about to scream, your daughter disappears
completely, collapsed into the small implosion of your phantom egg.

THE MORTICIAN'S DAUGHTER DIES EACH NIGHT

When my father laughs my stomach scatters in the wind like hay.
Lying on my back can turn the bed into a coffin since I'm his

only child and the kisses dead women give him mushroom on his face
at night. All poison, all frost, his *¡Buenas noches!* freezes my blood

as he bids goodbye to the members of the wake, every one a tapering light.
This house is a village of pressed suits, starched gowns where sleep

comes so heavily the eyes anchor at the lower skull. Girls must act adult
in frowns, their dimples pulleys suddenly. I understand the gesture,

my mouth no different when my father sneaks in through the dark.
How they weep for me, the moaning caught between the stones of teeth.

If they could breathe they would expel the scent of father's brilliantine.
Once I saw a dead girl twitch her finger and I cried and cried

for the helpless motion of resistance come too late. I hear him walking
in. I stop my heart. One skill I've mastered here is playing dead.

THE MORTICIAN'S MOTHER RETURNS

Neighborhood gossips had it all wrong,
this terrible parable with her face stamped
on it. What a scene: the bicycle fugitive leaving behind

the flatline of her murdered marriage across the dirt road.
Her son, marked fate, had no choice but to anoint
the dead, people said, as they continued to blame her,

woman secretly rooted in her garden. When the old house
was leveled and the earth raked clean, out with the truth
in the shape of spokes, handlebars, ribs and a hunting dagger's

jagged grin. The culprit, long-dead, the son, long-gone.
What comfort, sack of broken bone and knots of hair,
can you offer your prodigal boy now? He pulled out hearts

for a living but didn't keep a single one for her.
How fitting that she should reappear the same week
the mortician gets buried. They are always trading places:

he on wheels, now she; she under the knife, now him.
What heartbreaking dance, the mortician's mambo in which
mother and son never meet. Back to the ground she goes

without a soul to mourn her. The priest takes pity and kisses
her grave with his feet. *Until kingdom come,* he says.
What's a death day but another rusty nail worming its way

out of wood? She'll know when to rise again when
the dogs whistle through the larvae tunnels in their throats.
What warm winds will spiral out of the pumiced bone.

Tunes. The potatoes sing them when they leave the earth.
Never does a skull bob out of its hiding place without
tragedy in its teeth. Woman, back to the ground. Don't speak.

The Mortician's Goddaughter Versed in Lust

Just when I had long outgrown those late-night
        seizures in my hand, those involuntary impulses
return to make my fingers twitch like the tips of twigs
        after the bird leaps off the branch—

what a crafty little devil, bouncing back all
        feathered and ticklish, jittery with pleasure
when it finally finds its nest. The sheets become as damp
        as the sweaty shirts that cling to the backs of men

at the dance, and how I pity the girls who
        undress their lovers before sex.
When I started loving other bodies instead, allowing other
        temporary guests to mold their shapes inside my flesh—

a torso of my arm, a shoulder of my mouth, a waist
        or a buttock of my leg—I had no need
to concentrate my rapture to a single sticky place
        since every movement in my skin was slowing down

inside the vat of honey I was swimming in.
        Oh bath with tongue, oh alchemy of heat and bed.
The memory of so much sex enough to keep me sated
        in the quieter evenings of my third and final age.

So imagine my surprise when those possessions
        from my adolescence woke me up again, but in the guise
of scribbling from my pen. Not fancy or confession
        but something in the middle, like the mole that snuggles

in the space between my breasts, that glorious discovery
    that makes the men cry out, the women
shudder with anticipation or intent. It's more like poetry,

because it whistles through the paper like the weekend
    afternoons I summoned passersby from behind
the window's curtain. What wonder to seduce with sound,
    granting serendipitous fantasy—here a table

with rotating thighs, there a closet panting with exhaustion,
    there the eye of the voyeuristic clock bold and
looking to be satisfied with one pair of feet pointing at
    two opposite corners of the room,

three fingers always vanishing inside the cluster of
    four hands that motion slowly left, slowly right—
the capricious current of the underwater flower,
    five limbs comparing lengths and flexibility,

their competition sabotaged by the arrival of a
    sixth contender, seven escalating levels in the throat—
whimper, grunt, moan, sigh,
    whine, hum, groan, cry—oh, and if we're lucky,

thinks the grinning clock, we will spiral up the scale
    (and down again) a good
eight times, nine would be too much to ask,
    though not impossible since there was once a

record-breaking tenth, remember?
         Eleven minutes for a quickie; at least
twelve positions for a marathon. Now *why* would I write
         a thing like that, me who wears a garter belt to church

on Sundays, my best perfume to market,
         where tomatoes look as dazed as the tomato seller?
Blame it on my mother's poor choice for a compadre,
         none other than the legendary lover, the mortician,

whom the women always said would have his way
         with one, in life or in death—both,
if one was fortunate. And the rumor always was
         that he had fathered me, though I never did detect

any resemblance. But what does it matter
         anymore? I've outlived even the mortician's crazy
daughter (half-sister, if the hearsay is correct).
         If the mortician is my muse, then let him color

every word in ink as dark as pubic hair.
         Where to begin? Ah, yes, fittingly, at the little piece
of skin that stimulates imagination:
         I'll compose a poem to the mortician's scar.

ACKNOWLEDGMENTS

Bellevue Literary Review, Black Warrior Review, Diode Poetry Journal (online), *Electronic Poetry Review* (online), *Fishouse* (online), *Guernica* (online), *Hayden's Ferry Review, Heliotrope, Laurel Review, Luna, Painted Bride Quarterly, The Rogue Scholars Collective* (online), *The Superstition Review* (online), *Washington Square*

"The Mortician's Scar," "The Mortician's Daughter Dies Each Night," "The Mortician's Mother-in-Law Says Goodbye," and "The Mortician's Mother Returns" appear in *Poetry 30: Thirty-something American Thirty-something Poets*, eds. Gerry LaFemina & Daniel Crocker (DuBois, PA: MAMMOTH Books, 2005).

"The Girl with No Hands" appears in *The Poets' Grimm Anthology*, eds. Jeanne Marie Beaumont & Claudia Carlson (Ashland, OR: Story Line Press, 2003). Reprinted in *The Endicott Studio Journal of Mythic Arts* (online), Winter 2006, eds. Terri Windling & Midori Snyder.

"Mise-en-scène" appears in *Stranger at Home: American Poetry with an Accent,* ed. Andrey Gritsman et al (New York, NY: Interpoezia, Inc. & Numina Press, 2008).

With much gratitude to Idaho's Sun Valley Center for the Arts, Hailey Cultural Center, and to the Ezra Pound Association for the gift of a one-month residency at the Ezra Pound House, where an early draft of this book was completed. Thanks also to the Julia and David White Artists' Colony in Costa Rica, to the Hawthornden International Writers Retreat in Scotland, to the folks at le Chateau Lavigny in Switzerland, and to Queens College / CUNY for a timely two-year visiting position.

To my divas: Tayari Jones, Jayne Anne Phillips, Kimiko Hahn, Marion Ettlinger and Martha Rhodes—love. To Bhanu Kapil, D.A. Powell, and the poetry students of the Rutgers-Newark MFA program, hugs. And to the Advisory Circle of Con Tinta, strength.

Rigoberto González is the author of eight books of poetry and prose, and the editor of *Camino del Sol: Fifteen Years of Latina and Latino Writing*. The recipient of Guggenheim and NEA fellowships, winner of the American Book Award, The Poetry Center Book Award, and the Shelley Memorial Award of the Poetry Society of America, he writes a Latino book column for the El Paso Times of Texas. He is contributing editor for *Poets & Writers Magazine*, on the board of directors of the National Book Critics Circle, and associate professor of English at Rutgers-Newark, the State University of New Jersey.